JUST LOOK AT...
THE ANCIENT FAR EAST

Yonit and Alastair Percival

Macdonald Educational

Factual Adviser: Julia Hutt, Far Eastern
Department, Victoria & Albert Museum

Editor: Carolyn Jones
Teacher Panel: John Allen, Sam Chaplain, Tim
Firth
Designer: Ewing Paddock
Production: Rosemary Bishop
Picture Research: Diana Morris

Illustrations
Marion Appleton 29, 32–33, 34–35
Peter Bull 8–9
Peter Dennis/Linda Rogers 12–13, 14, 16T, 18,
19, 22–23B
Richard Hook 10–11
Graham Hutt, 15T
Louise Nevett back cover, 16B, 21, 22–23T, 31, 39

Photographs
BPCC/Aldus Archive title page, 19, 27, 31T
Bridgeman Art Library 36
Werner Forman Archive 23
Robert Harding Picture Library contents page, 21,
24B, 28B, 35BR, 37T, 42
Michael Holford 15B
Hutchison's Picture Library cover
Institute of History and Philology, Academia
Sinica, Taipei, 15T
Museum of Fine Arts, Boston 40–41
National Museum, Korea 31B
National Palace Museum, Taiwan 20, 25B
Tokugawa Art Museum 38B
Tokyo National Museum, photographs courtesy of
International Society for Educational Information,
Tokyo 35BL, 38T, 41T
Zefa 17T, 17B, 24–25, 34, 37B

Title page picture: A painting of Chinese children
flying kites.

British Library Cataloguing in Publication Data
Percival, Yonit
    The ancient Far East – (Just Look At)
    1. East Asia – History – Juvenile
        Literature
    I. Title   II. Percival, Alastair
    III. Series
    950
    ISBN 0-356-13217-X

How to use this book
Look first at the contents page to see if the subject you want is listed. For example, if you want to find out about Marco Polo, you will find some information on pages 24 and 25. The word list explains the more difficult terms found in the book. The index will tell you how many times a particular subject is mentioned and whether there is a picture of it.

The Ancient Far East is one of a series of books on history. All the books on this subject have a yellow colour band around the cover. If you want to know more about history, look for other books with a yellow band in the **Just Look At . . .** series.

A MACDONALD BOOK
© Macdonald & Co. (Publishers) Ltd 1988

First published in Great Britain in 1988
by Macdonald & Co. (Publishers) Ltd
London & Sydney
A member of Pergamon MCC Publishing Corporation plc.

All rights reserved

Printed in Great Britain by Purnell Book Production Ltd
A member of BPCC plc.

Macdonald & Co. (Publishers) Ltd
Greater London House, Hampstead Road, London NW1 7QX

CONTENTS

THE FAR EAST

This map shows the three countries whose history you can read about in this book, China, Korea and Japan.

This is the story of the peoples of ancient China, Korea and Japan. These three countries form the eastern quarter of the continent of Asia. This part of the world is called the Far East or, sometimes, the Orient. 'Orient' is an old word for sunrise. You may have noticed that the sun always rises in the eastern sky.

Let us put the countries on the map. The islands of Japan lie in the western Pacific Ocean. They form a curve facing the mainland of China. Korea is the long narrow strip of land, called a peninsula, which sticks out from the China coast towards Japan. Korea and Japan are both medium-sized countries. China is many times bigger.

Today, roughly a quarter of the world's population lives in the Far East. The Chinese, Koreans and Japanese belong to the same group of peoples as Eskimos and American Indians. Usually, their skin is yellow-brown. They have almond-shaped eyes, high cheekbones and black hair. The people of North China tend to be three to five centimetres taller than Koreans. Most Japanese are slightly shorter than their mainland neighbours.

Early and important civilizations sprang up in the Far East. Three oriental inventions changed the history of the world. Without the navigator's magnetic compass, the Europeans could not have launched their great voyages of exploration. Without paper and printing, books would have stayed rare and expensive. Without gunpowder and guns, armies would have continued to fight with swords, bows and arrows. Long ago, the Far East made many of the discoveries on which life in the modern world is based. In the West, for example, drilling for oil and natural gas is a recent development in the history of science and industry. But the Chinese were using iron-tipped bamboo drills to find gas deep within the earth's crust more than 2,000 years ago.

China is the oldest of the three nations. It was the first country in East Asia to invent writing and to use metal tools and weapons. From China, knowledge and ideas spread to Korea and Japan. The rulers of Korea and Japan followed the customs of the Chinese court. They modelled their cities and temples on Chinese plans. India was the only foreign country which greatly changed life in the Far East. The rice plant and the religion of Buddhism both came from India.

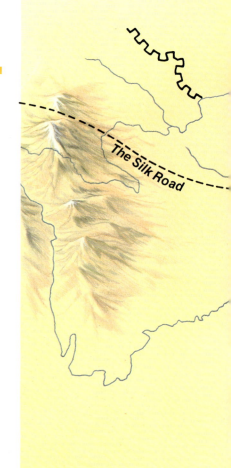

The Silk Road

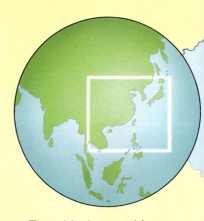

▲ The white box on this picture of the Earth shows the area that is covered by the large map above.

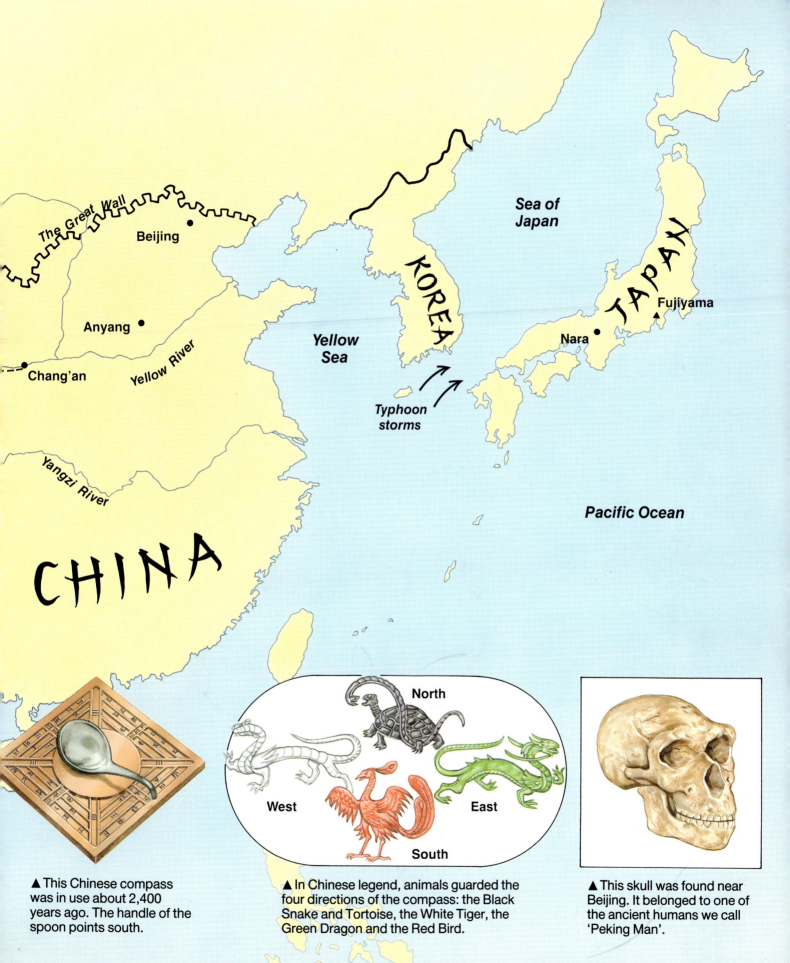

The Great Wall

Beijing

Anyang

Chang'an

Yellow River

Yangzi River

CHINA

KOREA

Yellow
Sea

Typhoon
storms

Sea of
Japan

JAPAN

Nara

Fujiyama

Pacific Ocean

North

West

East

South

▲ This Chinese compass
was in use about 2,400
years ago. The handle of the
spoon points south.

▲ In Chinese legend, animals guarded the
four directions of the compass: the Black
Snake and Tortoise, the White Tiger, the
Green Dragon and the Red Bird.

▲ This skull was found near
Beijing. It belonged to one of
the ancient humans we call
'Peking Man'.

9

The Arrival of People

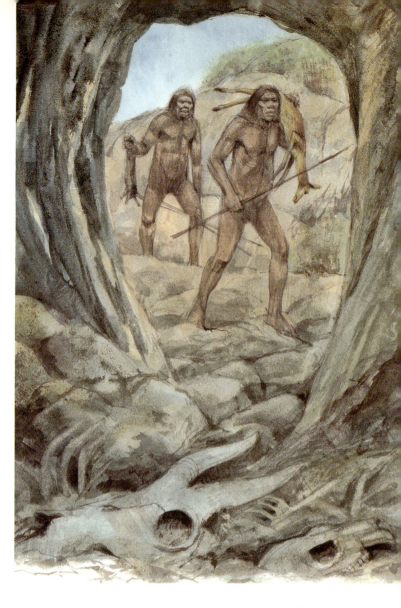

About twelve million years ago, human-like creatures lived in the foothills of the Himalayas. Scientists believe these were the earliest ancestors of people. They were called *Ramapithecus*. Unlike the ape, they walked on two legs. They were much shorter than us, probably less than 1.22 metres tall. A closer relation of modern people appeared in the Far East about half a million years ago.

Dragon Bone Hill rises to the south of Beijing, capital of modern China. In 1923, archaeologists found a tooth in a limestone cave in the hill. Lower down in the cave floor, they unearthed the bones of about forty people. There were also stone tools and animal bones, all half a million years old. It was a sensational discovery. At that time, these were the oldest human remains ever found. Scientists called the ancient people 'Peking Man'. ('Peking' was the old spelling of Beijing). They belonged to an ancient type of human called *homo erectus*, 'people who walk upright'.

'Peking Man'
These ancient people looked rather ape-like, but their arms and legs were just like ours. Their

▲ Half a million years ago, people only had three ways to start a fire. They could strike a spark from a flintstone, or rub two sticks together, or keep alight a natural fire started by lightning.

The chart below shows how people's skills developed in the Far East. ▼

500,000 BC

Peking Man lives in North China, using fire and stone tools

30,000 BC

Homo sapiens lives in North China, making jewellery of bone and shell

5,000 BC

Rice farming begins

The first pottery is made

1800 BC

Bronze is used for tools, containers and weapons

The first writing is used

700 BC

Iron is used for tools and swords

brains were only two-thirds as big as ours, but it is possible that they could speak a simple language. These cave-dwellers made useful tools by flaking lumps of stone. They also knew how to light a fire. Bits of charcoal and burned bone tell us that they may have been the first humans to cook their food. In the forests, they had to defend themselves against fierce sabre-tooth tigers, rhinos and elephants. They ate the meat of the horses, wild pigs, buffalo, antelope and deer which roamed the grasslands. These people may also have been cannibals. Archaeologists found human and animal bones in the caves which were all splintered. It looked as if people had broken them on purpose to suck the marrow inside.

'Homo sapiens'
We know nothing more of people in the Far East until about 30,000 years ago. Then, we know that more advanced people were living in the same

caves in Dragon Bone Hill. These were *homo sapiens* – modern humans like us. Archaeologists think that they evolved from the earlier, more primitive *homo erectus*. They looked much less ape-like and were more intelligent than 'Peking Man'. They drilled holes in animal teeth, stone beads and sea shells to make necklaces. This is the earliest jewellery found in the Far East. About this time, people began to look for new areas to hunt. Perhaps, also, they were curious to see what was on the other side of the next mountain. Wanderers from northern and central Asia drifted across to Korea and Japan. They could go all the way by land in those days. The Japanese islands of Hokkaido, Honshu, Shikoku and Kyushu were linked to the mainland until about 20,000 years ago. Even after the sea had crept between Korea and Japan, the waters froze in winter. So it would still have been possible to make the crossing without a boat.

CHINA, THE MIDDLE KINGDOM

For centuries, China and Europe knew very little about each other. China was hidden from the West by mountains so high that they were called the 'Roof of the World'. Few Westerners travelled there. No wonder the Chinese name for their country was the 'Middle Kingdom'. They thought they were at the centre of the world.

The Chinese have records of historical events which go back about 3,500 years. There were earlier civilizations in Mesopotamia and Egypt, but they died out. China's ancient language has survived until today. A thousand years ago, it was the most advanced country in the world. Engineers spanned rivers with iron suspension bridges. The Chinese invented paper and printing, and the magnetic compass. Their ships sailed around India to trade in Africa and Arab countries. Chinese scientists drew accurate maps of the stars and planets. Chinese doctors understood the circulation of the blood. The army used bombs and flame-throwers. The Middle Kingdom was also the most efficiently governed country on earth. Horsemen brought news to the capital from all parts of the vast empire within a few days. The officials who ruled the people, called civil servants, had to pass special examinations. It was not enough to have come from a noble family. The civil servants were all highly educated. They were trained to govern and promoted on merit.

Everything was on a grand scale. Large and beautiful cities were built. Roads were hung from mountain sides on beams dug into the rock. When the Emperor Yang ordered a canal to link the waterways of the north to those of the south, two million labourers went to work. The canal was 1120 kilometres long, 18 metres wide and 6 metres deep. It was part of a system of canals that was the finest in the world. They made it possible to move a lot of grain very quickly from one part of the country to another. Chinese historians tell us that, when the emperor travelled the country, his caravan of courtiers was 480 kilometres long. When he cruised the Yellow River, 80,000 men pulled his fleet of pleasure boats. The emperor's barge had cabins of jade and gold. Furniture was covered in tiger, bear and leopard skins. Musicians entertained the royal family on board.

Chinese civilization started 2,000 years before the countries of Europe. By the time science in Western countries began to catch up, China's development had slowed. One reason may have been that the rulers and civil servants of China did not welcome people with new ideas.

An imperial procession sets out on a tour of inspection. Villages along the way had to provide food and lodging.

The First Kings

The beginning of Chinese civilization is clouded by legends. For centuries no-one had any real evidence of events before about 1,600 BC, though story-tellers spoke of an ancient family of kings called the Shang. Then, in 1928, archaeologists found the ruins of a Shang city. It was a very important discovery. It proved that the legends were true and the Shang people had really existed. This is how it happened. Farmers near a town called Anyang kept ploughing up scratched animal bones. Chemist shops used them to make 'dragon bone'

medicine. Finally, a doctor realized that the bones were scratched with ancient writing. Archaeologists dug in the fields where the bones were found, and discovered the city. Its name was Yin. It is the oldest city we have found in the Far East.

Yin was founded by a ruler called Pang Geng nearly 3,500 years ago. The builders used elephants to help with the heavy work. Prisoners-of-war and animals were buried in the foundations as sacrifices to the gods. Yin was

◄ The Shang king and his ministers watch as the priest prepares to crack an animal bone with a heated stick. This form of fortune-telling was only used in Asia.

Chinese writing uses pictograms instead of an alphabet. The chart shows how modern characters developed from the early pictograms. For instance, the symbol for 'to walk' came from the outline of a crossroads. You can see some more Shang writing on the 'oracle bone' below. ▶

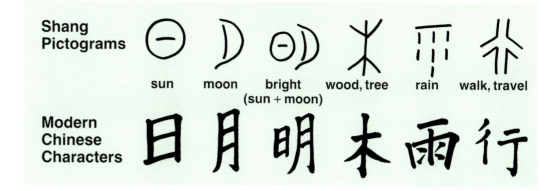

Shang Pictograms

sun   moon   bright (sun + moon)   wood, tree   rain   walk, travel

Modern Chinese Characters

日 月 明 木 雨 行

carefully planned, with a wall around the outside. The palace was in the centre. Around it were wooden buildings for priests and advisers. The rest of the people lived in thatched houses.

'Cradle of civilization'

Yin was built in a valley of the Yellow River. This area is sometimes called the 'cradle of Chinese civilization'. Here, China's first farmers cleared the land for crops. Archaeologists have found stone ploughs which are more than 6,000 years old in the Yellow River Valley. In the same area, centuries later, the Shang kingdom produced the first bronze tools. Shang workshops made spades, knives, axes, arrowheads, hoes and fish-hooks. The Shang people were traders. They took bronze tools to distant parts of Asia and exchanged them for tin, lead, salt, tortoise-shells and jade. Shang traders became so widely known that a merchant is still called a 'Shang man' in China. Shang nobles led large armies. Enemy prisoners became their slaves. When a lord died, his slaves were buried with him. Magnificent vessels of bronze were placed in the tombs. These vessels were used for sacrifices to ancestors and gods.

'Oracle bones'

When the Shang king wanted advice, his priests consulted Di, the chief god. The king might ask if there would be a good harvest, or if he would win a war. The priests cracked animal bones and tortoise-shells with heated rods. The pattern of cracks showed the god's reply. The question and answer were scratched on the bone. It was these fortune-telling or 'oracle' bones which the Anyang farmers had found. They showed the earliest Chinese writing. Experts were able to read the bones. They proved that the fifteen legendary Shang kings had really lived.

◀ This is an 'oracle bone' of tortoise shell. On a bone like this, Chinese scientists found the earliest written record of a nova, or exploding star.

About 1500 BC, Chinese metalworkers were the most advanced in the world. The Shang used bronze bowls for religious ceremonies. A few were in the shape of animals, like this tiger holding a man's head in its mouth. ▼

A Million Soldiers

The Shang kings were overthrown by the Zhou people in 1027 BC. The Zhou ruled for hundreds of years, but in the fourth century BC other states began to fight the Zhou and each other for control of China. This was the Age of the Warring States.

In 221 BC, final victory went to the Prince of Qin (pronounced Chin), who conquered the six rival kingdoms. For the first time, all China was one country. The 'Tiger of Qin' became the First Emperor, Shi Huang Di, ruler of the largest empire in Asia. He is said to have led 'a million armoured soldiers, a thousand chariots and ten thousand horses to conquer and gloat over the world'. Along the northern border, the First Emperor completed the largest fortification the world has ever known, the Great Wall of China. He hoped it would protect his empire from invasion by horsemen from the north. The wall was 3,200 kilometres long. Many workmen died of cold and hunger while they were building it. The peasants called it 'the longest cemetery on earth.'

The Great Wall
The Great Wall had a staggering 25,000 forts and watch-towers. Guards signalled for help at signs of enemy movement. To report an emergency at night, a sentry lit a fire of dry wood on top of the tower. When the next post saw the flames, it also lit a fire to pass the message along. During the day, the sentries would burn wolves' dung to make smoke. For ordinary messages, they waved red or blue flags. A signal could be sent 480 kilometres along the wall within a matter of hours. In quiet times, the soldiers were kept busy with patrols or crossbow practice. Powerful crossbows were their main weapons. Every morning, the guards inspected the ground at the base of the wall. It was smoothed over with sand so that an enemy scout would leave footprints.

◄ Crossbows were fearsome weapons. Qin archers could fire bolts up to 200 metres.

The Great Wall of China is the only man-made object that can be seen from space. ►

This shows how the Great Wall was made. Earth was stamped into a wooden frame before the outside was covered with stone. ▼

▲ The 'Terracotta army'. Over 7,000 life-size figures have been found so far. Every one's face is different.

Sometimes, the soldiers had to make bricks of mud, baked in the sun, to repair the wall. Each tower kept a store of builder's tools, stocks of spare arrows, and jars of water and food to last two months.

The first empire

The First Emperor, Shi Huang Di, unified his vast country. He made new roads and gave orders that the wheels of carts were always to be built the same distance apart. That meant a cart or a carriage would never be too wide for any road and could travel everywhere. He also made everyone use the same weights and measures and the same writing system. The First Emperor was ruthless. He executed scholars who disagreed with his ideas, and burned their books. As soon as he became emperor, Shi Huang Di put 750,000 men to work to build his tomb. Artists placed thousands of lifesize clay soldiers, chariots and horses around the burial chamber. These pottery figures are known as the 'terracotta army'. When the emperor died, the workmen who knew the secrets of the tomb were buried with him. Trees and grass were planted on top to make the tomb look like a hill, and hide it from grave-robbers.

Peasants and Emperors

Chinese society was like a pyramid. The emperor was on top, with nobles and civil servants to advise him. Next came peasants and craftsmen, soldiers and merchants. When war or rebellion shook the pyramid, the emperor sometimes toppled down. This was how the Qin royal family lost the throne in 206 BC. The man who took over, Liu Bang, was a poor villager's son. He and his supporters had rebelled against the cruelty of the Qin government. The building of the Great Wall, for example, had caused great hardship and loss of life among the peasants. After seven years of war, Liu Bang won control of the Chinese empire.

Although he could not read or write, Liu Bang was a wise ruler. He founded the great Han dynasty which ruled for more than four hundred years. A dynasty is a royal family.

The 'Son of Heaven'

The Chinese called their emperors 'Sons of Heaven'. They believed that Heaven gave each emperor a 'mandate' or right to rule. If he treated the people badly, as the Qin emperors did, this mandate would be taken away and given to someone else. So Liu Bang was regarded as a true 'Son of Heaven', even though he took the

An emperor listens to a girl playing a Chinese lute. Hundreds of court musicians and dancers were trained in the palace at Chang'an.

Peasants like these hardly had one day's holiday in a year.

throne by force. The great Han dynasty was itself overthrown in AD 220. In the next thousand years there were three major dynasties, the Sui, the Tang and the Song.

The emperors of China were cut off and protected from the common people. Sentries in watchtowers guarded the gates of the palaces. Hundreds of slaves waited on the emperor day and night. Women spent years embroidering magnificent silk robes that the emperor might wear only once. Throughout his reign, thousands of labourers worked to build his tomb. When he died, the emperor was buried with the same luxury and security he had known in life.

▲ The seed drill, which was invented in ancient China, made farming more efficient. It trickled out seed in straight lines.

Peasant life

The empire of China depended on peasants. In the Han age, there were sixty million Chinese. Most were peasants. They served in the army as well as growing food for everyone. They built the roads and dug the canals that criss-crossed the land. A Han official wrote that poor peasants wore the skins of oxen and horses and ate the food of dogs and pigs. The average peasant supported a household of five people. In good times, they could afford pigs, perhaps a goat, and an ox to pull the plough. The animals would share their earth-floored cottage. From sunrise to sunset, every day of the week, the peasants and their children worked in the fields. After paying tax to the emperor and rent to the landlord, the peasants might not have enough to live on. Sickness would put them in debt. If they borrowed money, they might have to repay twice the amount. Sometimes peasants had to abandon their fields and become beggars.

The Family

Family life was very important in China. A famous teacher called Confucius described how families should behave. Confucius was born about 550 BC when frequent wars caused much misery. He spent his life looking for ways to ease the suffering of the people. At first, few paid attention to him. But after his death his writings were studied in schools all over China. Everywhere, temples were built in his honour. His ideas have greatly affected the Chinese way of life right up to the twentieth century.

Confucius taught that members of a family should be loyal to one another. 'Treat other people as you would like them to treat you,' he wrote. Children had to respect and obey their parents.

Chinese law allowed an angry father to demand the execution of a son or daughter who disobeyed him! Confucius said that the same respect and loyalty should exist between rulers and subjects. He laid down a 'ladder of obedience'. The Emperor came before your family, old people before young ones, and men before women.

Men and women

In China, grandparents, parents and children all lived under one roof. It was the same in a palace

With his wife and children, a son kneels to show respect to his parents. This was done morning and evening in wealthy homes. ▼

Chinese beliefs and customs were based on the teachings of three men. Lao Zi wrote a book called 'The Way of Virtue'. Buddha, which means 'awakened one', was an Indian prince who founded the religion of Buddhism. Confucius was a wandering scholar who made rules about how people should treat one another. ▶

 Lao Zi

 Buddha

 Confucius

as in a mud-and-straw hut. The oldest man in the family, usually the grandfather, was head of the household. At meal times, he was served first. The eldest son or eldest daughter's husband sat or knelt next to him.

The women cooked and presented the food. They did not eat with the men. Confucius taught that women must obey men. A single girl had to do as her father said. When she married, she had to obey her husband and his parents. If her husband died, she had to obey her eldest son.

A wife's duty was to bear sons. Daughters were not welcomed. This was because a daughter went to live with her husband's family when she married. She could not look after her own parents in their old age. A son, on the other hand, did not leave home to marry. He and his wife respected and cared for the son's parents all their lives.

'Golden Lily' feet

A thousand years ago, a cruel custom began. In wealthy families, daughters had their feet tightly bound in early childhood. The bandages bent the toes under and limited the growth of the foot. It crippled the girls, but their tiny feet and small steps were considered beautiful. The ideal foot was called the 'Golden Lily'. It measured less than 8 centimetres from heel to toe. Compare that with your own feet, and you can see how painful it must have been. Crippled feet kept women at home. Farmers' wives and daughters worked in the fields and had some freedom, but the wives of scholars and nobles rarely went outside. A lord's wife died in her burning house rather than break a rule about not going out at night. Rich peasants and nobles had as many wives as they could afford. If the first wife became jealous of the second, her husband could divorce her.

▲ A court dancer was the first to wrap her feet in bandages. It became fashionable to bind the feet tighter and tighter. Soon all wealthy girls, and even a few of their servants had to have bound feet. The binding became so severe that girls could no longer dance. They could barely walk.

The Story of Silk

Silkworms are kept on large trays and fed day and night with mulberry leaves. They spin cocoons in seven days. The cocoons are boiled in water, unwound, and then spun into thread. The silk thread is woven into cloth. It takes about 1,600 silkworms to produce half a kilo of silk. ▶

picking mulberry leaves

Silk was a Chinese invention. For centuries, no-one outside China knew how silk was made. Chinese law said that anyone who told the secrets of silk-making to a foreigner would be punished by death.

The making of silk is skilled and delicate. A tiny caterpillar, the silkworm, lives on the leaves of the mulberry tree. The silkworm produces a long unbroken thread which it wraps around itself to form a cocoon. Only the Chinese knew how to raise silkworms, unwind their thread, and weave it into cloth.

The Silk Road
Ancient Romans knew China as Serica, which means the 'land of silk'. Elegant Roman ladies would pay high prices for light silk dresses, which were so cool in summer. When the Roman Emperor Julius Caesar entered Rome in 60 BC, bright sheets of Chinese silk shaded the streets from the sun. From China, traders carried the silk west along the Silk Road. It was a long, hard journey. The road ran from the capital, Chang'an, across endless deserts and mountains, to Syria and the waters of the Mediterranean. About once a year, a great caravan set off for the West. The

A camel caravan sets off along the Silk Road. No merchant travelled the whole distance. Goods changed hands many times along the way. ▼

trays of silkworms

a silkworm on mulberry leaf

boiling cocoons

a cocoon

weaving silk

camels were loaded with skins, iron, lacquer, rhubarb and cinnamon, but mainly they carried silk.

The Chinese could not keep their precious knowledge to themselves forever. In the sixth century AD, a group of monks managed to smuggle some silkworm eggs to the West. They hid them in a hollow stick and risked their lives to outwit the Chinese authorities. The making of silk was no longer a secret.

Merchants and money

The earliest travelling merchants exchanged goods for cowrie shells, but by 1500 BC people were using metal coins. They were shaped like spades or knives. Round coins of copper appeared about 900 BC. They had a hole in the middle so that the coins could be gathered on a string. In AD 1000, Chinese traders began to exchange goods for paper money. The Chinese people called it 'flying money', because it could easily blow out of your hand.

In Chang'an, wealthy merchants could afford to live in three- and four-storey houses. Beds were curtained with fine silks. Some very rich families kept their own singers and orchestras of bells, drums, flutes and lyres. Their horse-drawn carriages gleamed with gold and silver fittings. For entertainment, they loved tiger fights, gambling, and dog or horse racing. Weddings were an occasion to show off. Men and women dressed up in red badger or fox furs. The banquets went on for hours with one tasty dish after another.

Embroidered silk badges like this showed the rank of court officials. A dragon with five claws was the emperor's symbol. ▼

Marco Polo and the Great Khan

The Chinese had always feared invasion by their enemies north of the Great Wall. Early in the thirteenth century, the Mongols conquered the other northern tribes. The Mongols were wandering shepherds. They were superb horsemen who could ride in freezing temperatures for weeks on end. In battle they often defeated much larger armies by their speed and ferocity.

In 1212 the Mongols charged through the Great Wall and swept southwards. Over the next sixty years they conquered the whole of China and Afghanistan, Persia and South Russia. By 1271 their leader, Kubla Khan, ruled the largest empire the world has ever seen. It stretched from the Mediterranean to the Sea of Japan.

'Master Million'
While Kubla Khan was declaring himself emperor in Beijing, a young Italian was beginning an extraordinary journey to China. His name was Marco Polo. He was seventeen years old when he set out in 1271, but he did not see his home again until he was middle-aged. On his return, Marco wrote the first book about the unknown Far East. Many European readers could not believe the incredible sights he described. They thought he was exaggerating. People joked that the book was full of 'a million of this and a million of that'. So they called him Master Million.

Today, it is hard to imagine the terrors and hardships of Marco's journey into the unknown. It took six years to reach China, six years of hunger and thirst, snowy mountains and scorching deserts. Marco was well rewarded, however. Kubla Khan liked Marco and took the young man into his service. No-one knows exactly what job Marco did, but Kubla Khan sent him on many

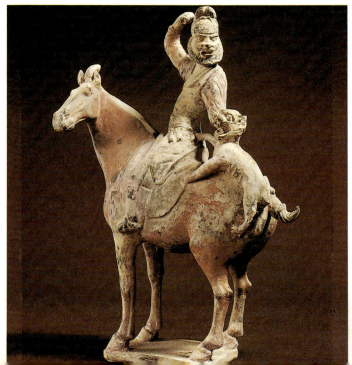

missions to distant parts of China. Marco saw many wonders on his travels. He was astonished by the widespread use of coal, paper money, dried milk, and fireworks. The Chinese had invented gunpowder some 400 years before Marco's arrival. By Marco's time, the Chinese had learned to make deadly bombs and cannons as well as fireworks.

Kubla's court

Marco wrote in his book that 10,000 bodyguards sat down to monthly banquets at the Great Khan's court in Beijing. The palace had 400 rooms painted gold, silver and blue. The roofs were tiled red, yellow and green 'so that they shone like crystal'. According to Marco, Kubla Khan kept lions for hunting bears and matched leopards against deer. When Kubla Khan was out hunting and saw a tree he liked, elephants would pull it up, roots and all, for gardeners to plant at the palace. Marco may have exaggerated a little bit. But he really saw so many wonderful things in China, it is not surprising.

Marco and other Europeans could not understand how the Mongols governed hundreds of millions of people in China and Asia. They thought the Mongols were fighters, not rulers. In fact, the Mongols copied the Chinese system of government. Kubla Khan ruled like a Chinese Emperor or 'Son of Heaven'. In China's long history, the foreign invaders became just another dynasty, the Yuan.

▲ Kubla's palace may have looked like this great hall, built on the same site in Beijing many years later. It is now called the Forbidden City.

◄ Chinese works of art like this pottery horseman fascinated the Mongols, who made nothing like this themselves.

The Mongols loved hunting. In this painting, Kubla Khan is on horseback, but sometimes he hunted from the back of an elephant. ►

KOREA, LAND OF THE MORNING CALM

A Korean garden party. The wide brims of the men's hats are typically Korean.

In the beginning, says Korean legend, a tiger and a bear begged the god Hwanung to change them into human beings. Hwanung gave each animal a bundle of herbs and twenty pieces of garlic. The god told them to eat only these and to stay out of sunlight for one hundred days. The tiger was impatient and disobeyed, but the bear did as it was told and was turned into a woman. She married Hwanung and they had a son, Tan'gun. He became the ancestor of the Koreans.

We cannot say precisely when people first arrived on the peninsula. Tools of stone, wood and bone have been found in all parts of the country. One site has been dated by archaeologists as 50,000 years old. Around 800 BC, bronze tools were introduced from China. People began to live in villages and to bury their dead. They dug underground tombs for their rulers. It required organization. Each burial chamber was roofed with huge stone slabs. Large numbers of people must have worked together to cut and transport stones of this size.

In ancient times, the people were split up into many tribes who fought each other. But they also had to band together against the Chinese, the Mongols and the Japanese. After an invasion by land and sea in 108 BC, the Chinese army formed a colony called Lelang in the north of the country. To the south, the tribes slowly gathered into three kingdoms. They were called Paekche, Koguryo and Silla. The Age of the Three Kingdoms produced skilled craftsmen, artists and metal workers. The Japanese sometimes paid whole villages of Koreans to move to Japan to pass on their knowledge and skills. Before the eighth century AD, few Japanese could write and Korean families kept all their early records.

Silla was the smallest kingdom, but it became the strongest. After seven centuries, the Chinese were driven out. In 660 AD, Silla attacked Paekche. The king made his last stand against the Silla army in a hilltop castle. On one side of the castle, the hillside dropped straight down to the Kum River below. The cliff is called the Rock of the Falling Flowers. It is said that three thousand ladies of the Paekche court threw themselves from the cliff top rather than surrender. Silla defeated Koguryo, the third kingdom, eight years later. From north to south, the whole peninsula was now governed by Silla. For the first time in history, the people were one nation. It became a golden age, famous for its brilliant art, magnificent temples and huge palaces.

'Little China'

Twelve hundred years ago, Silla's capital of Kyongju had a population of one million people. Its rulers lived in wealth and splendour. Kyongju was the fourth largest city in the world. Its broad avenues were as straight as arrows. The grid-pattern street plan was modelled on Chinese cities. Roofs were made of grey tiles, often with animals and flower designs. Pagodas towered above the city. Monks and scholars travelled to China to study. They brought back knowledge of Chinese culture. The kingdom was proud of its nickname, 'Little China'.

Women and dress

Women sometimes wore trousers so they could ride more easily – Silla was famous for its horses. However, noble ladies usually wore long, full skirts. White was a favourite colour for clothes. Ordinary women were not permitted to wear red, because that was the queen's colour. Her winter clothes were made of embroidered red silk. The wives and daughters of nobles did not show their hands in public. They covered them in a kind of sack hanging from the end of their sleeves, even when they used a fan. Girls wore their hair in one

Large buildings in ancient Korea, like this wooden temple in Kyongju, had upward-curving roofs. The style was copied from China. Unlike private houses, temples were colourfully decorated. ▼

A wealthy Korean family at home. Men ate separately from the women and children. They even lived in different rooms in the house.

long plait dangling down their back. Married women plaited or coiled their hair up on top of their heads. It may seem strange to us, but women did not have names of their own. A girl was so-and-so's daughter. When she married, she was so-and-so's wife.

Korean homes

Most houses faced south to catch the sun. Homes were built of wood. There was not much furniture, and people usually sat or knelt on the floor. The houses had sliding doors with panels of rice paper that let the light through. In the chilly winter season, houses had under-floor heating. Hot air from the kitchen fire was piped all round the house. The floor was covered with light straw mats. People did not sleep in beds. The family rolled out mattresses at bedtime, one mattress per person. Young children slept with their mother until they were big enough to have their own

mattress. Pillows were filled with wheat husks. They must have felt very hard.

Eating

From wall paintings in ancient tombs, we know the people of Silla ate with spoons and chopsticks. In wealthy households, there were chairs and tables. Royalty and nobles had plates and bowls made of gold, silver or glass. The ordinary people took their meals sitting on the floor. They used dishes of pottery, wood and brass. Rice was the basic food for all, as in other countries of the East. It was served with vegetables such as cabbage, radish, cucumber, aubergine, ginger and lotus root. Usually, only the rich ate meat. In a peasant's house, there was seafood for special occasions – seaweed, oyster, shrimp, clam and crab. Chestnuts and pine nuts were put in big jars and buried underground to keep until the next summer.

Koryo

The lords of Silla had great wealth, but the peasants stayed poor. Many farmers paid tax both to the king in the capital and to the lord of the nearest castle. Hardship drove some to leave the land and become bandits. The people began to revolt as lives of luxury weakened their masters. A rebel leader called Wang Kon founded a new state in AD 917. It was called Koryo, from which we get the name 'Korea'. The last king of Silla surrendered peacefully in AD 935.

Strict rules for life
Wang Kon and his immediate successors were wise rulers. They built 'righteous granaries' to store grain so that they could feed the poor when harvests were bad. They introduced China's system of paid civil servants. These men were selected by examinations for their ability to govern the country. But only the sons of noble families could occupy government posts. You could tell the rank of an official by his clothing.

The highest wore purple, the second dark red, the third bright red, and the lowest green.

Everyone's job and the way they lived was fixed at birth. Children of slaves automatically became slaves. Marriage outside the same class was not allowed. Commoners were called 'yangmin' or good people. They were chiefly peasants. The land they farmed belonged to noble families. Merchants and craftsmen were also commoners. Below them were the 'low born'. They were the hunters, sailors, mineworkers, butchers, potters and basketweavers, travelling entertainers and slaves. The low-born did not pay taxes or serve in the army.

Koryo had many festivals. For rich and poor, New Year's Day was a great holiday. Everyone lit paper lanterns and burned lamps of oil in seashells. For a girl, a bright flame was a sign that she would find a good husband in the New Year. On the

◄ On the fifth day of the fifth moon, after spring planting, farmers took a day off for sport and feasting. Here, some men are watching a bout of judo, which was introduced to Koryo in the twelfth century.

◄ Silla kings had vast wealth. This is one of the ten golden crowns dug up from royal tombs near Kyongju. Kings were buried with gold rings on their toes, gold necklaces and gold belts.

▲ Women relax beside a stream at the May festival of Tano. Swinging contests were traditional on this holiday. From her hair, you can tell that the girl with the long plaits is unmarried.

summer festival of Tano, boys and girls washed their hair in water boiled with flowers. Children with ribbons in their hair swung from trees on long ropes. People enjoyed wrestling matches. On Snake Day, country folk avoided combing or cutting their hair. If they did, snakes were sure to nest in their homes.

The Mongols invade

The people of Koryo always feared invasion from the north. They built a wall along the northern frontier, which was finished in 1044. It was no better than a defence than the Great Wall of China. In the thirteenth century, the Mongols rode into Koryo and devastated the land. Finally, the Mongols agreed to make peace. But in return, Koryo kings had to marry Mongol princesses. Every year, they had to send large quantities of gold, silver, silk and grain to the Mongol Emperor in Beijing. A thousand women had to go to China each year to marry Mongol soldiers. Koryo was occupied by the Mongol invaders for more than a century.

JAPAN, LAND OF THE RISING SUN

Ancient Japan was a poor country. It was always difficult to grow enough food. The islands are mountainous, and only a tiny area can be farmed. There is almost no flat land. People lived in small valleys or plains between the mountains. The country's symbol is Fujiyama or Fire Mountain. It is a volcano. Until 300 years ago, Fujiyama often threw out burning rock. People had to keep well away from its gentle slopes. The earth's crust is thin in this part of the Pacific. Often, the land trembles. Every five years on average, there is an earthquake strong enough to damage buildings. Violent tropical storms called typhoons sweep in from the ocean in autumn. It is no wonder that only the Mongols ever tried to invade Japan. Storms destroyed their ships. The Japanese called the typhoons which saved their country *kamikaze*, or the 'divine wind'.

Japan lies 800 kilometres off the shores of China. The Chinese called these mysterious islands Jih-pun. It means 'origin of the sun' or Land of the Rising Sun. Marco Polo wrote about the islands in his book, but he called them Jipangu. The modern name 'Japan' may come from Marco's spelling of the Chinese word. The Japanese learned about rice, metal, writing, money and silk from Korea and China. The islanders did not just copy foreign ideas. Usually, they developed them to suit the needs of Japan. For example, Japanese poetesses found Chinese writing slow and complicated to use. They simplified the letters until their written language looked quite different from the original. The traditional dress for Japanese men and women, the kimono, also came from China. The kimono, which is still worn today, is based on Chinese court costume of the seventh century. The Japanese designed lovely patterns and colours that made the kimono one of the world's most beautiful garments.

The first Emperor of Japan was called Jimmu. People believed he was the great-great-great-grandson of the Sun Goddess. Legends say he began to rule in 660 BC. But historians claim a more accurate date is the fourth century AD. Jimmu was a chief of the southern island of Kyushu who defeated the clans of central Japan. He built a palace on the Yamato plain and celebrated his conquest with ceremonies in honour of the Sun Goddess. Jimmu now called himself the 'tenno', the Emperor of Heaven. Since then, there have been 126 emperors and they have all come from the same family. For centuries, Japan's great lords fought each other for land and for influence at court, but they never took the throne. The Japanese still celebrate festivals which mark the day that Jimmu became emperor, 11 February, and the day he died, 3 April.

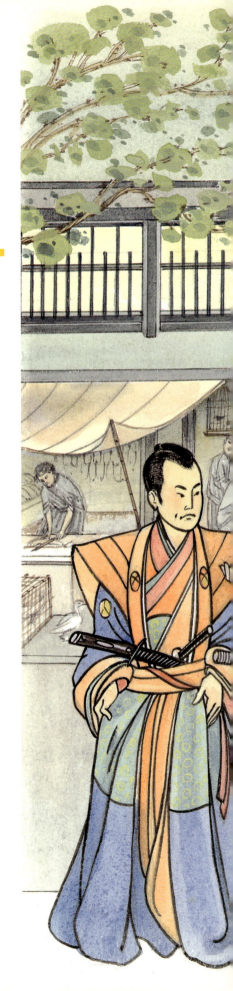

A busy street in Japan. Wheeled transport was rare, and porters carried most goods.

The First People in Japan

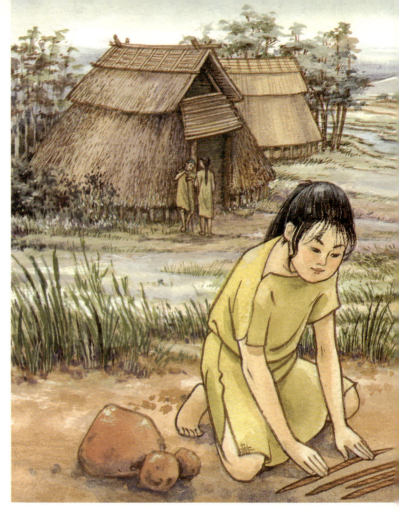

Elephants and giant deer as big as horses roamed the forests of ancient Japan. Wild pigs provided people with meat, skins and fat. Their long bones were made into tools. People gathered walnuts, mushrooms, roots and wild grapes to eat. They also hunted mountain lion, monkeys and bear with traps and bows and arrows. From the bones that archaeologists have found, we know they were careful to kill only male deer. The hunters avoided killing females and young so that the herds could breed.

Stone Age Japan

The remains of Stone Age settlements are scattered all over Japan. Homes were usually grouped in a horseshoe shape. Their slanting roofs of thatch or bark rested on wooden posts. About 2,300 years ago, these hunters and fishermen learned how to grow rice. They began to build granaries to store food. The clusters of thatched shelters grew into large villages. Weapons and tools of bronze and iron replaced stone axes and bamboo arrows tipped with bone. The first metal was probably brought from Korea, but iron was being made in Japan by the first century AD.

These early inhabitants were known to the Chinese as Wa, which means small people or dwarfs. From their skeletons, we know the men were about 1.55 metres tall. The women were several centimetres smaller. A Chinese record of AD 297 gives us a picture of their way of life: 'They eat with their hands from wooden trays and platters. Men live with men, women with women. Squatting or kneeling shows respect to their leaders. Boys and men tattoo themselves. They also paint their bodies pink and scarlet with rice-powder'. Traces of this body-paint have been found on clay burial figures.

In those days a sea voyage or a journey into the lands of other tribes was a dangerous adventure. To ensure good luck, the travellers chose a person staying at home as the 'fortune-keeper'. As long as they were away, the fortune-keeper was not allowed to eat meat, wash, comb his hair or touch women. If the journey was successful, he was rewarded with fine gifts. If the travellers met with disaster such as a shipwreck, the fortune-keeper was killed.

Mirror, jewel and sword

On the Yamato plain of central Japan, an organized system of society began around 1,600 years ago. The chieftain became a priest-king. He led a religion that worshipped the Sun God. The ruler carried the symbols of royalty, a metal mirror, a jewel and a sword to represent the sun, the moon and the lightning flash. In a land of volcanoes and earthquakes, it was not surprising that men and women worshipped the forces of nature. Each mountain had its own god. There were river gods, rain gods, wind gods. Every village had a shrine to the rice god, Inari. This ancient religion had no name. In the sixth century AD, the Japanese began to call it Shinto, 'the way of the gods'.

▲ In a Stone Age village, a young girl is rolling out strands of clay for her mother to coil into a pot. This is how pots and jars were made before the potter's wheel came to Japan.

◄ Flat, waterlogged fields are needed to grow rice, but level land is rare in Japan. The problem was solved by cutting hill-side terraces which could be flooded.

This clay tomb figure, called a *haniwa*, tells us how a soldier looked in sixth-century Japan. Metal bands reinforce his leather helmet. The iron breast-plate is tied with bow knots. ►

▲ Each Shinto shrine and holy place has a wooden 'torii' or 'bird-perch'. In Japanese legend, it was birdsong which persuaded the Sun Goddess to come out of her cave and light up the world.

Buddhism in Japan

In the sixth century AD, a new religion arrived in Japan. This was Buddhism, which had spread across the Far East from India. In Japan, it started a bitter struggle between Buddhists and the followers of Shinto. The emperor was High Priest of the Shinto religion. Under him, nobles served as chief priests in Shinto temples. It was their greatest honour. They were afraid that Buddhism would weaken their influence at court.

The trouble began in AD 552, when a Korean king sent a gift to the Japanese emperor. It was a gold and copper statue of Buddha. Some of the Japanese nobles warned that the native Shinto gods would be angry. The Soga clan, however, welcomed the new religion. The Emperor did not know what to do. Finally, he gave the statue to the Soga clan. Three young nuns, one only eleven years old, were taught to pray to Buddha. Then a plague broke out in the city. Followers of Shinto blamed the statue. The poor little nuns were whipped in a market-place, and the statue was thrown into a canal.

Buddhism is accepted

In AD 585 a new emperor, Yomei, came to the throne. He believed in Buddhism as well as Shinto. Some clans still opposed Buddhism, but the Soga defeated them in battle. With the Emperor's approval, the Soga sent the young nuns to Korea to study Buddhism. They brought back priests, monks, carpenters, painters and sculptors. Soon there were Buddhist temples alongside Shinto shrines all over Japan. Colourful Buddhist ceremonies were held when an Emperor was ill or when the crops needed rain. In AD 749 Emperor Shomu put up a colossal statue of Buddha at Nara, the capital. It still stands there. The figure is 16 metres high and is made of 500 tonnes of copper, tin, lead and gold. The great

▲ Long after Buddhism was accepted in Japan, the Soga continued to fight with other clans. Here, the Soga brothers Goro and Juru set out to avenge their father, who was murdered by another clan.

hall that houses the statue is the largest wooden building in the world.

The new religion also encouraged the use of writing. The Japanese had no writing system of their own, so they learned to write their language in Chinese characters. Scribes copied Buddhist scriptures for the temples. One Emperor personally copied a holy text in gold letters for his favourite shrine. In the eighth century, Buddhists brought wood block printing to Japan. Carvers cut the letters on wooden blocks. They brushed ink over the block and pressed a sheet of paper down on top. Now, most people could afford to have the scriptures in their homes. In 764, Japanese monks printed one million copies of a Buddhist picture.

By the tenth century, Shinto and Buddhist temples owned large areas of tax-free land. They had to defend their property against each other and against jealous nobles. In this violent age, monks were trained to use weapons. Monks from different temples fought one another and even raided the capital city.

▲ Gold leaf once covered this giant Buddha at Nara. Japan's first gold mine was found in the year that the statue was finished. Emperor Shomu led national rejoicing.

◄ The Todaiji temple at Nara is the headquarters of Buddhism in Japan. The gilded 'horns' on the roof are charms to protect the temple from fire.

'Daughters of Heaven'

Women often ruled in ancient Japan. An early traveller from China called Japan the 'queen country'. He wrote of Himiko, queen and sorceress of the Tribes of Wa. Her name means 'daughter of the sun'. She ruled over the island of Kyushu. The queen was said to live in a heavily-guarded fortress served by one thousand women and only one man, her brother. Himiko never married for fear of losing her magic powers.

The empresses of Japan

The first empress of all Japan was Jingo, who lived about 1,600 years ago. She was expecting a baby when her husband died. Jingo took the throne. A legend says that she carried a stone weight on her stomach to delay the birth of her child. She led an invasion of Korea and, on her return, gave birth to the next emperor, Ojin.

The long skirts of tenth-century noble ladies swirled out around them. The outer robe hid many layers of kimono. ▼

◄ Some of the oldest folk music of Japan originated in the rice fields. It gave a rhythm to peasant women planting seedlings.

▲ Here a noblewoman sets out on a journey in a special carriage called a palanquin. She has armed guards to protect her against bandits.

Some emperors deliberately passed the throne to a daughter, not a son. But a woman could have great influence at court without becoming empress. The clever Soga family often married their daughters to royal princes. The future emperor was likely to take advice from his mother and to favour her clan. Often, the new emperor was only a child. He was advised by an older man who was called a regent. These regents often came from the mother's clan. They held the real power. Emperors became weak, and ruled in name only.

In the eighth century, an empress fell in love with a monk. The monk wanted to become emperor, and the empress agreed, but the court was horrified. The ancient royal family, descended from the Sun Goddess, had almost given away the throne! The monk was banished and the court never again allowed a woman to rule.

Famous women
Ladies of the court had little to do. They spent their days dressing up for splendid ceremonies and writing poetry. The emperors' wives surrounded themselves with clever women. These court ladies competed with each other in fine writing. Sei Shonagon was a lady in waiting to the Empress Sadako and a famous author of the eleventh century. In her Pillow Book, she said girls studied writing, music and twenty volumes of poetry. The most famous books in ancient Japan were by women. A noblewoman known only as the Mother of Fujiwara Michitsune was one of the great poets. She kept the first diary of a Japanese woman. It was a sad tale because her husband neglected her. Lady Murasaki wrote the *Tale of Genji* about life at court. It was the world's first novel.

A young woman even won fame as an archer. Hangaku joined in the defence of her family's castle at Echigo. In April 1201, dressed as a boy, Hangaku stood on the tower of the castle and shot every soldier who attacked her. Finally, she was taken prisoner and brought before the enemy general. A soldier, impressed by her beauty and courage, asked to marry her. The general thought the request was extraordinary – 'she has no woman's heart,' he said – but he agreed.

Samurai and Shogun

In the twelfth century, Japan was torn by civil war between the great clans. Many people died of hunger and disease. The war was finally won by General Yoritomo of the Minamoto clan. His military chiefs took over the government from the emperor's lords. In China, people looked down on soldiers. In Japan they became the strongest and most respected part of society. These warriors were called samurai, which means 'one who serves'.

The samurai
You could recognise a samurai by the two swords in his belt, one long and one short. The blades were the strongest and sharpest ever made. Before heating the steel, the swordmakers prayed for the blessing of the war god Hachiman. They wore white robes like priests while they hammered the metal into shape. A sword was the symbol of a soldier's honour. A samurai who parted with his sword was disgraced.

The samurai made war into an art. For example, there were just four correct targets for the long sword – the top of the head, the wrist, the side and the knee. No samurai would be proud of wounding an enemy in the wrong place. The samurai had their own special code of behaviour called 'the way of the horse and the bow'. They valued fighting skills and loyalty to their masters. A samurai was not afraid of death. It was better to die than to be taken prisoner.

Story-tellers sang about samurai deeds. The most famous story was about General Yoritomo's younger brother, Yoshitsune. Yoshitsune was a

brilliant soldier, handsome and popular. He won the final battle in the civil war for his brother. This was the sea-fight of Danoura in 1185. General Yoritomo became jealous of Yoshitsune's success and the younger man had to go into hiding. General Yoritomo ordered his soldiers to find him. Rather than surrender, Yoshitsune killed his wife and child and took his own life. He had obeyed the samurai code, 'better to die with honour than to live in shame'.

The shogun
By 1185, General Yoritomo and his Minamoto clan were all-powerful. Yoritomo set up his

Samurai of the Minamoto clan storming the Sanjo Palace in 1159. The former emperor Goshirakawa was taken prisoner. The palace was set on fire and destroyed. ▶

▲ A wooden statue of the first shogun, Yoritomo, wearing formal court costume. The statue may have been carved during Yoritomo's lifetime.

headquarters at Kamakura, a village far from the capital. The emperor gave him the title of 'shogun' or commander-in-chief. The shogun appointed military governors in every province. In this way, he controlled the samurai, who now held all the power in Japan.

The emperor was still on the throne, but he had no real authority. A 'feudal' society began. This means that men fought for the local lord in return for his protection and the right to farm his land. From now until the nineteenth century, the true rulers of Japan nearly always belonged to the warrior class.

Books and Places, Time Chart

Books to read

A Closer Look at Early China, Boase, W., Hamish Hamilton, 1977
The Ancient Chinese, Lai Po Kan, Macdonald, 1980
See Inside an Ancient Chinese Town, Unstead, R.J., Hutchinson & Co. Ltd., 1979
Great Civilizations: Ancient China, Knox, R., Longman, 1978
Everyday Life in Early Imperial China, Loewe, M., Batsford, 1968
China, Land of Discovery and Invention, Temple, R.K., Patrick Stevens Ltd, 1986
Japan, the Land and its Peoples, Hoare, S., Macdonald 1975

Places to Visit

British Museum, Great Russell Street, London. Displays of ceramics, bronzes, jade and tomb furnishings from China, Korea and Japan. The Education Service provides worksheets on Chinese Animals and Monsters.

Science Museum, Exhibition Road, London. The collections include oriental scientific instruments, clocks, junks, and a large display on traditional Chinese medicine.

Victoria and Albert Museum, Cromwell Road, London. The museum has one of the largest collections of Chinese court costumes in the West and beautiful examples of oriental silks.

Pollock's Toy Museum, Scala Street, London. Toys and games from the Far East include shadow puppets and kites.

Ashmolean, Beaumont Street, Oxford. A good collection of Far Eastern art.

Fitzwilliam Museum, Trumpington Street, Cambridge has an outstanding Korean collection.

Burrell Collection, Pollokshaws Road, Pollok Country Park, Glasgow. A large collection of Chinese ceramics, especially Tang pottery. Chinese bronzes and jade items, and Japanese woodblock prints.

Royal Museum of Scotland, Chambers Street, Edinburgh. A large Chinese collection including ceramics, bronze, jade, costume and sculpture.

Durham University Oriental Museum, Elvet Hill (off South Road), Durham. Chinese ceramics, jade animals, Japanese weapons, and the only Chinese bed in any European museum!

Bristol City Museum and Art Gallery, Queens Road, Bristol. Permanent displays of Chinese art. Collections of costume and paintings and Japanese prints can be seen by appointment only.

If you are living in or visiting North America, you can find many Far Eastern collections. For example, the Metropolitan Museum of Art in New York, the Cleveland Museum of Art, the Nelson Atkins Gallery in Kansas City, the Amery Brundage Collection in San Francisco and the Royal Ontario Museum in Toronto, Canada.

◄ An Imperial dragon from a tiled wall in Beijing.

	China	Korea	Japan
BC 500,000	'Peking Man'		
30,000		First settlers	Hunters and cave-dwellers
10,000–7,000	Farming and silk-making begins		
5,000	Rice cultivation begins		
2,000	**1500** Shang dynasty begins Bronze Age **1027** Zhou defeat Shang	Farming begins	
1,000	**700** The first use of iron		**660** Crowning of the legendary 'First Emperor'
300	**221** Qin conquers all China **214** Great Wall is finished **202** Han dynasty is founded	Bronze introduced from China	Farming develops Society becomes more organized
200–100		Iron introduced from China **108** China conquers the north of Korea. The Three Kingdoms form in the south.	Bronze, then iron, introduced from Korea and China
AD 100	Paper used for writing		Japanese clans send embassies to China
200	**220** Fall of Han dynasty Buddhism is introduced from India		Himiko rules in Kyushu
300		**313** The Chinese are defeated **372** Buddhism introduced	Jingo rules in central Japan
400			Chinese writing system is introduced
500	Sui dynasty reunites China		**552** Buddhism is introduced The Soga clan becomes the strongest
600	**618** Tang dynasty begins Golden age of literature	**668** Silla defeats the other two kingdoms	The first Buddhist temples are built
900	**960** Song dynasty begins Gunpowder is invented Magnetic compasses used	**918** Koryo dynasty begins **935** Koryo defeats Silla	
1000			Golden age of literature
1100	**1127** Mongols invade north China		Civil Wars **1192** Yoritomo becomes shogun
1200	**1215** Mongols take Beijing **1271** Kubla Khan becomes emperor of China, and Marco Polo sets out for the East	**1231–5** Mongol invasion **1239** Koryo surrenders to the Mongols	**1274** and **1281** Mongols invade Japan but are defeated

Word List

The Analects The book in which Confucius described his ideas for living.

Archaeologist A person who studies the past by looking for objects which people have left behind. Archaeologists search for clues about the way people lived in the past. They may dig in the ground for bones and objects, or study information gathered by other experts.

Beijing The capital of China. Western people used to spell it PEKING, but BEIJING is closer to the sound of the Chinese name.

Bronze A metal made from a mixture of copper and tin. It is hard and can be made into efficient tools and weapons.

Buddha The ancient Indian prophet who founded the religion of Buddhism. He preached meditation and detachment from worldly possessions. Buddhists believe that people are reborn again and again until they achieve a perfect life.

Caravan A number of traders and pack animals travelling together.

Ceramics Pottery, china and porcelain items. Usually, they are shaped from a clay mixture and hardened in an oven.

Cinnamon A sweet spice used in cooking.

Civil servant An official who is paid to help govern the country.

Civil war A war between different groups of people in the same country.

Cocoon A sheath or covering made by caterpillars, who live inside it while they change into butterflies. Silkworm cocoons are made of fine silk thread which can be unravelled and spun into cloth.

Continent A large area of land bounded by sea. It may contain many different countries.

Dynasty A royal family. A dynasty can last for centuries with each ruler passing the throne to a son or daughter.

Earthquake A violent shaking and splitting of the ground caused by movements inside the Earth's crust. In Japan earthquakes happen often.

Empire The area controlled by one ruler, containing a number of countries or kingdoms. The ruler is called an emperor or empress.

Fortification A wall or other strong defence.

Homo erectus The scientific name of an ancient species of human beings, our ancestors. It means 'people who walk upright'.

Homo sapiens The scientific name for modern humans like us.

Imperial To do with an empire. For example, the 'imperial palace' is where the emperor lives.

Legend A story about ancient people or things. Legends usually include incredible or magical events.

Magnetic compass A device which helps sailors and travellers to find their way. A needle or rod in the compass always points north/south.

Mandate The right or permission to do something.

Marrow The soft edible middle part of some bones.

Peninsula A long strip of land sticking out into the sea.

Pictogram A simple picture used as writing instead of letters and words.

Ramapithecus Ape-like creatures, the ancestors of modern people. They lived millions of years ago in the Himalayas.

Shang The oldest Chinese dynasty, who ruled the Yellow River area in the second century BC.

Shinto The oldest Japanese religion, called 'the way of the gods'. It grew from the worship of nature and natural forces. Even after Buddhism came to Japan, Shinto remained important. Many people believed in both.

Shogun The military chief who ruled over all the samurai in Japan. In theory he was a subject of the emperor, but in fact the shogun usually held the real power.

Stone Age The time before people learned to make tools and weapons of metal. They used flints and sharp stones for cutting.

Suspension bridge A bridge which hangs from cables fixed to tall towers. A suspension bridge can span deep gorges where traditional bridges could not be built.

Terracotta A mixture of clay and sand which is shaped into pots, statues or tiles and baked hard. It is usually red-brown in colour.

Volcano A weak place in the Earth's crust from which melted rock and ash pour out in an eruption.

Index